Latter Day Parables
and Other Revelations

Latter Day Parables and Other Revelations

Georgia Beyard

VANTAGE PRESS
New York

Cover design by Polly McQuillen

FIRST EDITION

Published by Vantage Press, Inc.
419 Park Ave. South, New York, NY 10016

Manufactured in the United States of America
ISBN: 0-533-15110-4

Library of Congress Catalog Card No.: 2004099323

0 9 8 7 6 5 4 3 2 1

To Andy and Paul Beyard,

to The Wednesday Writers,
and to
Betty Walter,
John Hutchinson,
and Sister Ruth Miriam Carey,

Without them there would have been no book.

Contents

Latter Day Parables
and Other Revelations

Compensation

When the palsied man could not enter
the house where the healer was curing
multitudes, the palsied man's friends
sawed a hole in the roof and lowered
him to the healer. He was healed.
It rained all night.
The rugs were ruined.
The homeowner sued the healer.

Wedding

Everyone wanted a bottle of the new wine
and the name of the caterer. No one
noticed the bride.

Parkinson's

Arranging my parts on the mattress
like pieces of chicken on a platter,
unable to bear bone on bone,
sweating and sleepless at three A.M.
I remember Mr. Boyd, ex-Naval officer,
hero of the South Pacific, five years before I met him.
I first heard his shuffle, slide, shuffle in the hall
of the old Marine Hospital. Sometimes, he leaned
    forward
in a lurching trot, barely kept upright by his pretty,
uncomplaining, white-haired wife.
Mr. Boyd trembled like a pond in a bitter wind,
ceaselessly, clown grin stuck on his pink, patent leather
    face.
I was young then and knew my body never would betray
    me.
Now I have become Mr. Boyd.

The next day, desperate, I plead with
    St. Therese of Lisieux,
sender of roses to those she promises to heal,
"Send me a rose from your heavenly garden
that I may know that I will be healed."
I stand in the doorway wrapped in my Protestant
    skeptic's prayer,
believing and not believing,
Just then, the yardman drags by the last dead rose bush
he yanked out of the ground that morning.
Smiling he clips two red roses from the plant's thorny
    throat
and hands them to me.

Baseball and "Boheme"

Row houses,
sinking wooden porches,
every house alike,
Brown lawns, five by twelve,
every lawn alike,
a few green whiskers
sprouting at the edges.
A dry September.
Down the block
the same hydrangeas
in front of every house
their blooms
blue-puffed baby heads.
Inside one of those houses,
Saturday Dad,
a different Dad
from workday Dad,
a cold one on the coffee table,
lights up
smokes away the afternoon.
TV on. Sound stilled.
White balls whip by
in the bullpen.
On the radio
Saturday opera
loud.
Two ragged lovers
search for a key
in garnet darkness.
The batter hits
an impossible three-two pitch.
The ball

hangs for a moment,
painted sphere
in painted sky.
Then the ball arcs
over the stands
to the street
as Mimi and Rudolpho
soar in duet
their souls loosed
by love.
"Christ," Dad says. "It's enough to make you cry."

Journey

Shuffling
my way to seventy-five.
I find along the route
wise young doctors,
most of them women, but a few of them, men,
innocent as acolytes.
They carry clipboards and ballpoint pens.
Freed of the weight of words,
I offer little anecdotes:
loss, death, grief
in twenty second takes, smiling;
no tears in the telling any more.
And they like that,
that I'm so casual and cool
with nothing left to lose.
Smiling,
I play the part
of the silver-haired old lady,
wanting nothing
but a cup of coffee,
cream and sugar.

The Russian

He leaned against the rusted gate of my heart until it
    swung open and let him in.
I was an old woman, even then.

I found him standing next to a restaurant on the corner
where every morning in every season I waited for the bus
    to take me to work.
He looked hungry. I gave him a five-dollar bill to buy a
    meal.
He took it without a thank you and went into the
    restaurant,
and sat down at a table. At first, the white-haired waitress
    didn't want to serve him,
but he smiled a little blue-eyed smile. The waitress
    brought him eggs.
I boarded the bus.
The next morning he was waiting for me.
He took me by the hand.
I did not go to work.
We sat in my house the rest of the day.
He told me in broken English how he came here in a
    broken boat
from St. Petersburg. I was so ignorant I didn't know
    whether St. Petersburg
even fronted on a sea that led to the Atlantic.
I did not want to know. He had a blond stubble and a
    mouth redder than usual
for a man and tangled yellow hair. He told me he was
    descended from a Tsar's son
and I believed him because he was tall and walked like a
    man brought up in palaces.

I gave him apple cake and mugs of tea
and my father's gold watch and my dead husband's
      overcoat
because it was cold and he had a blue-eyed smile.

He told me his parents died young and he was raised by
      an uncle
who beat him and starved him and I believed him
      because I was a reader of Russian novels.
I let him in whenever he knocked and we heard from
      time to time melancholy Russian music on the
      classical radio station. His eyes would fill with tears.
      I believed the tears were real because the music was
      real. If he said something I did not understand, I
      believed it was Russian because it came out of his
      full red lips.

I listened.

I gave him the key to my house.

I gave him the key to the house.

To Whom It May Concern

That thing inside the elegant birdcage of your bones,
ragged and raw
will not die.
It is the bird with bloody beak
singing to the deaf fools
he loves.
It is the lover ready to immolate himself for love.
It is the dog that licks the boots of the one who kicks it.
It is the hammer building the ladder to climb the tower
where the princess dreams in her enchanted sleep.
It is the river rushing the body to the sea.

You give me your heart.
I'll give you mine.
We won't know the difference.
Our hearts are the same:
bloody flags we carried in so many battles.
We have worn our paper dunce caps far too long.
Let us cut out hearts from them
on which to write and then erase
vows of everlasting love.

We wish our hearts
were bouquets of dark red chrysanthemums,
fragrant and soft,
tied with purple ribbon,
withered, but worthy
of saving
for a little while.

Advice

As the donkey bore his burden into the holy city
he lifted his head and murmured,
"Master, let me turn back
and carry you away."
But the mob was too loud.
The ass was not heard.
Besides
who listens to an ass?

Dogwood

I want to write about the white dogwood.
It grows against my neighbor's white wall,
a blaze of beauty, careless as fire.
But I tremble, my arms move without my will.
Between this world's mysteries
and me,
confusion of the flesh.
The dogwood gleams in the west window,
its flowers, scattered green circles,
its pale petals, white leaves, indented,
flecked pink.
This glory grows straight up,
pinched against the wall.
It survived years of lightning's careless flashes,
last summer's bitter drought,
last winter's stone heavy snows,
Its branches shiver with the weight of birds,
but its wood is hard and heavy.
I will find a little boat
not far from here,
and, trembling, row across a river,
soon.
The dogwood will stand.
Legend says
dogwood formed the cross.

Watermelon Man

Summer 1935.
Watermelon man.
Grin splits his coffee-colored face. Paint peeling cart
Jangling rusty horse
blinkered, almost blind.
"Red ripe," the watermelon man
calls down the sun heavy street.
Black teeth in the cut red melon mouths.
"Red, red, red to the rind,"
melon man cries.
Heat bends the horse's
fly spotted back.
On a door
a long wreath
flecked with white flowers,
a white ribbon for a child.
Watermelon man
stops his song,
takes off his straw hat,
the horse huffs and stops.
Boys, barefooted,
dressed in hand me downs,
too big for them
throw a ball with one hand,
hold up their pants with the other.
A woman calls from a window,
"Hush, boys, hush. You know
there's a death in the street.

Watermelon man,
bring a melon here,
a little one, red and sweet
I'll trade you,
water for you,
water for your horse.
I don't have a penny or a dime."

Encounter

This morning
standing at the salad bar
of the supermarket
trying to cram red cabbage into an already overstuffed
plastic box
I felt the familiar
sway of the drug induced involuntary muscle spasms
take over
and move me in the same
old unwilling dance
to mad music
only I can hear
but I got my salad anyway
turned
saw an old guy
an aging cherub
haloed in silver hair
grinning.
"I saw you do that
shimmy shake," he said.
I tried to explain.
"No," he said,
"That was a beautiful thing."
He kept on grinning.
I grinned, too.
As they say
it's all in the eye of the beholder.
Anyway
there's a special
place in Heaven
for men who love women.

Valentine's Day

You are gone,
your dates are forgotten.
I keep sending Valentines.
No reply from you.
In the corner of the yard
where you planted crocuses
there is only ivy,
green as garden snakes,
even in February.
Deaf as I am,
I hear the splash the moon makes
swimming in evening's
purple water.
Tonight, the moon is a white arm
rocking you.

I gave your clothes to your brothers,
even your shoes.
They would not take your Air Force overcoat.
For months, it hung in the closet,
heavy as a hanged man.
Finally, I crushed
it into a black plastic
trash bag, dragged it to the curb.
All night, the trash bag gleamed
in the light from the street lamp.
You did not come to claim the coat.
I know. I did not sleep.

Blind as I am,
instead of stars,
in two more days,
I will see the moon's
black and white balloon face
bump from roof to roof
I will send you
one more Valentine
and try to tell you one more time
how the moon
will drag a cloud of pale hair
behind her into dawn,
and how, the first birds ascend,
cut patterns in the sky
with beating wings.

Who? Me?

The Roman official washed his hands.
The rest of us gave him the soap and water
and voted him back in office
time after time.

Unkie

. . . never had a name.
He was "Unkie" to his nieces, nephews—
"Buddy" to everybody else.
Fortyish bachelor,
lost a lot of jobs,
lived with his mother
in a second-story apartment,
begged his mother for "two bits,"
a quarter, fifty cents
for beer. Some days, a dollar.
Worked in the asbestos mill,
coughed all night long,
rolled his own cigarettes
from a little packet of tobacco
with a drawstring he pulled
shut with his yellow teeth.
He had a rack
wrapped around his neck to hold his harmonica,
blew in it, strummed an old guitar,
sang his country blues.
Hunted with his nephews
gave his pretty nieces
rings.
At forty-eight he married
a West Virginia bottled blonde, Sophie.
He got sick suddenly
with lung disease.
Sophie visited him in the hospital
almost every day until his sisters
and his mama scowled her and her
hillbilly high heels
out the door.

Sophie collected his insurance.
Two thousand dollars.
But Unkie had a real fine funeral—
wreaths of roses from the nieces, nephews.
The mortician gave him
a hair cut,
trimmed his black moustache.
Unkie
was almost handsome
in his big bronze casket.

Veteran

The old man curses, sobbing out farewells
to friends long dead. Alone, he hears them call.
His glucose tendrils root him in his hells

like ropes that hang in tower heights to bells.
Those bells have tolled him tombward. Still they toll.
The old man curses, sobbing out farewells.

He dare not dream what hope the cross foretells
that nails dead Christ in plastic to the wall.
His glucose tendrils root him in his hells.

No other hears the shrieks from smoking shells
cascading in the minefields of his skull.
The old man curses, sobbing out farewells,

and sitting out the siege the clock compels
him to endure without escape, for still
his glucose tendrils root him in his hells.

No longer conqueror of citadels,
instead a captive in a hospice stall,
the old man curses, sobbing out farewells.
His glucose tendrils root him in his hells.

Magnolia

One

Its buds split,
litter lawn and walkway
with fat, popped, velvet
mouse coats.
In the highest branch
the mockingbird, in his own gray mouse suit,
mutters
variations of his ancient melodies,
rehearsing
for nesting
under
the plump
fish belly sky.
I will take off
my gray galoshes,
stroll away
in slippers sewn
from mauve and ivory
petals.

Two

Early this morning, struggling to scratch out some kind of
      poem,
I mulled and muttered and stewed over metaphors,
      rhythms, rhymes
Everything scurried away. Nothing would stay,
not even one small simile.

Certainly no song.
Then I stuck my head out the door, saw that God
once again was sitting in the crook of the tree in the
 frenzy of the breaking open blossoms.
All day he has been humming tunes by Bach and the
 Beatles.
When I go out to see him in the tree, He says, "I am the
 living God."
And I say, "Yes!"

2003 Christmas

"I won't have a Christmas tree this year," you said.
Where is the fourteen-year-old boy who five times
hung lights from the eaves of the house
in biting cold
with fingers frost blighted
and five times blew the circuit breaker?
Each time the house for a few seconds
glowed like a Vegas strip club.
At last, you strung the little Japanese maple
in the front yard with red and green electric flowers.
It bloomed three winter weeks
in mists or rain or under a satin moon.
White dots dropped down
like movie snow
on Christmas Eve.
There was a war on the other side of earth.

War goes on.
They do not call it war.
Young men have learned
to walk with their brides
on the latest model prostheses.
The youth whose face caught fire and collapsed
says he's still the same inside.
Canned taps echoes in the graveyards.
Folded flags lie in the laps of widows
and mothers.

Deck the halls.

Transformations

When her eighty-year-old mother's face
had been molded by the mortician
into an unwrinkled blank, my friend
pushed and pulled on that smoothness
until the loved lines and sags of life
reappeared.
I don't know how true that story is.

When the surgeon bore a hole
in my skull to introduce the electrodes
that would stop the body's dreadful dancing,
the brain said, "No!" and seized.
And so I lived and saw the sun again.
But I said
"Let the hearse roll up as an ice cream truck,
trailing fifties tunes, bubbling with balloons.
I'm ready for a ride."

I said, "Here's my blue dress. Burn my body in it."
If the surgeon wants my brain,
let him have it. Maybe he can find its motor.
It forgot its stop-start mechanism
Its engine erased itself. In my kitchen, my feet
stuttered to a stop. I froze in corners, caught like
a thief on a video tape. On the street I danced
the puppet's crazed ballet, wanton and unwilling.
My bones floated to the surface of my skin,
ready to rearrange themselves outside my skin.
It was time to fly away,

Now my soul clings to a power line
chirping in a sparrow's throat.

Of Angels

The women, early that morning,
came to the tomb and saw that the stone
had been rolled away.
An angel gleamed in the darkness.
He spoke. They heard.
The women led the angel home.
He was so young.
He had flown all night.
His wings were torn.
They gave him bread and cheese there in the garden.
The barren fig tree bent down
with sudden heavy fruit.

Fourth of July

Of Antietam I remember rain
a shadowy bridge
Of Boston blaring traffic
brick
Of Gettysburg statues
rearing horses
men with raised swords
terrible sun
the cry of crows
Of Fredericksburg
old houses shuttered
boarded up shops
Of Savannah
stillness and Spanish moss
Sherman's headquarters closed
it was Sunday
Of Baltimore the fort
where the bright banner waved
through smoke
Of Washington
Lincoln silent in stone
Of Virginia
Arlington
endless markers
blurred in snow

Letter Found in a Drawer after Her Father's Death

April 17, 1927
Portland, Oregon

Dear Mama,

The train came in yesterday.
Spring across the country.
I hardly remember any of it.
I don't know this town,
It's not like Union Bridge.
I dropped around to see Rose.
Her Daddy was sitting on the porch.
"Son, don't marry Rose," he said.
Rose was sure surprised to see me.
She still has that long red hair.
There was no sky I saw across the continent
as blue as her eyes.
She smiled when I recited Bobby Burns.
Send me some money, Mama.
I'm going to marry Rose.
Your son, Joe.

Retrospect

When it's time
our families will buy us a box
to store us in the earth
out of sight, as is seemly.
We will fill that box
just as we filled the boxes
of our days, neatly.
No need for room to turn in.
No need for room for anybody else.
We made life's choices
as we chose our shoes, for fit and comfort.
Instead,
we should have sailed our leaky boats
in search of pirate treasures
and vanished cities under the sea.
We should have danced
in the moon white ballroom of the sky.
We should have let our lovers drink our heart's blood.
We should have let them burn our souls to ashes.

Cat

jumps straight up
to a shelf five feet
from the floor.
For a moment
she makes of air
an ordinary stair.
At three eighteen A.M.
she knows just where to place her purr on your pillow
and so denies the devil
a doorway to your dreams.
On the porch she places gifts,
mouse morsel, broken butterfly.
Washing her face, she smiles
her smooth assassin's smile,
crimps her mouth,
like Pharaoh's
mummified favorite.
She floats her tail,
a question mark in fur
over her disdainful back,
disappears,
then suddenly returns disguised,
a ghost with Nefertiti's eyes.

Recognition

When after three days, he returned
his followers did not know him.
Three days in hell
have changed many another lesser man.

Mother's Day

Looking out a window,
black and white with winter
my mother sits in the lobby
of the Saint James Hotel
Baltimore in a float of smoke
and music, a small woman
pearled, suited in the manner
of ladies in 1955.

She had called from Oregon.
I, her daughter, twenty-five
agreed to meet her here.
She has ridden the long,
long train from Oregon
as I did, age three,
1933, alone. Maybe
a Traveler's Aide was with me.
There must have been.
I remembered Mary, big hipped
in black and hatted like a cop.

I go down to Mother's hotel,
get off a yellow bus.
Wind. Snow whirl. Snow
skim on sidewalks. Night.
In the hotel I see a pale blue woman
at a table smoking.
I say, "Are you Ruth?"

She has had so many husbands.
Her letters, short, far apart,
arrive each time with a different
return address, a different
last name.

She says, "Yes," I see
nobody I ever knew.
She wants me to go west
with her, live with her.
She'll send me to school.
I say, "No." I'll go back
to my clerk's job in the hospital;
hope for a husband.
Years after my father's death
I find in a book a photograph
taken in Columbus, Ohio.
I was born in Columbus.
The woman in the picture
saucy in a twenties haircut,
smiling, young, beautiful,
with avid eyes thrusts
her head slightly forward.
I think she may be my mother.
I don't know, and now
there's no one left to ask.

Love in Another Season

Remember when
we climbed those stairs again
and yet again
to that high room we lived in
when
you were the first man I loved,
I was the first woman you loved
and ours was the only Eden
in an ever after wintered world?

Then, each day,
dawn unloosed its scarlet, purple, yellow flags.
The red maple lit up like a fire
just beneath our window.
Startled sparrows flicked from burning branches—
ashes from its blaze.

We kissed each other's tender lips.
And tenderly we took our time.

Mechanic

When the air conditioner mechanic came in the door,
I fell in love with him at once.
Who would not who had a heart?
He had the nose of a statue of Augustus,
the bearing of a ballplayer
who has just pitched a perfect game,
the eyes of a Leonardo angel.
He moved like music.
"You have a nice home here," he said.
I said, "You haven't seen the cobwebs
in the corners."

Cashews

Salivating like a dog I stood
on the oily floor of the Nut Shoppe
on Lexington Street in Baltimore
with my friend, Edna.
We were buying an eighth of a pound
of cashews, all we could afford,
to take to the Century Movie Theater
on the same downtown street
where we watched two lovers
shoot each other to death in the badlands
of some brown, gray and sandy Western state,
he in spurs and cowboy hat and dusty cowpoke pants
and she in peasant blouse off the shoulder and
    dirndl skirt.
Bullets bounced and pinged off the gray rocks.
The sun went down. They were still shooting each
other and their blood gleamed in the twilight.
Even at sixteen, Edna and I knew that love
more often than not is war and war to the death.
But we devoured our cashews and accepted that
as part of the price we would be happy to pay
for the caresses of some crazed, lean cowboy
as long as he was crazy for us.

Years later at a dinner on Gibson island in the home
of a renowned Hopkins professor, drinking Martinis,
trying to look sophisticated and older than twenty
I and the other guests, the professor's clerks and his
interns and their wives, we were offered cashews
in huge wooden bowls to eat with our drinks before
    dinner.
We took handfuls of them, devoured them. They were
    salty
and sweet and I remembered the killer in the movie, how
at the end he crawls to his lover and shoots her dead.

Now it is Christmas and for the last time I will serve
a Christmas dinner in this house.
I will buy cashews and cashews and plenty of wine and
    pour
and pour wine and eat cashews, maybe for the last time,
and think of the salt and sweet of doomed love.

Ascension

When the shepherds and the grape tenders
saw the young man rising to heaven
they were sure The Roman Circus Company,
    Incorporated
was giving a preview
of its latest show.
The shepherds and the vineyard tenders kept on working.

After Words

We would like to bring her down to the garden
in her wheelchair, roll her in the sun
to where the brown rabbit
nibbles clover. Stiff with fear,
only his hunger keeps him here.
He is no bigger than a child's fist.
His ears point this way and that
with too much listening.
But we can never bring her to the garden again.
She has gone where Jesus in his white
magician's cloak pulls rabbit after rabbit
out of his tall top hat,
plump rabbits, white and black and gray
with storybook twinkling noses.
She will hold the smallest one
in her hands
and feed it flowers.

Elephants

Two old circus elephants, Shirley, Jennifer,
retired, now together in an iron-barred
barn, bend the bars to reach each other,
break through.
Twenty-five years ago, Jennifer was
an infant, mothered by Shirley.
Separated soon after Jennifer's birth,
now rejoined, they remember,
twine trunk to trunk, walk in step
in Carol's meadow, where the sun
has tossed yellow ribbons on the new grass.
They throw their giant shadows down like blankets,
roll in joy in a cloud spattered pond.

Baseball Snapshots

Pitcher, holding up his gloved
and ungloved hands together—
pious praying mantis—
contemplating murder.

Catcher's glove, leather bivalve,
snapping shut.

Umpire, masked,
dark garbed Greek chorus,
grunting Fate's decrees.

Shortstop, second baseman,
first baseman
dance the double play
ballet.

Magician in the outfield
stretching
snatches an almost homer
throws it through
early summer stars.

Bus People

To the city, to the mad ward
of the famous teaching hospital,
traveling with my talismans,
the silver earrings from the sons,
the Testament my husband
carried in the War, I ride
the bus marked "River View."
Outside, red streaks of morning
splatter by.

A crown of curls with a woman
underneath hobbles up the aisle,
plops down next to me as though she
has been hunting for me all her life,
pulls her story out like a pair of glasses
from a handbag;
how she landed in Plymouth, England,
nineteen forty-two, a pilgrim in reverse,
met, married, and lost her husband
in a year. "His ghost was the only
child I ever carried."

The tall black goddess in thrift store
rayon opposite flings out her conqueror's
smile, shows us where a white scar
wanders on her skull under her new
 black velvet hair. "This is where they
dug out the tumor. I'm Darlene."

She and I get off the bus, walk down Greene
Street in the dazzle of a Dutch painter's
afternoon. On the corner, boom box jazz,
drumbeat, whoosh of cymbal like a sigh.
Men we pass stare at Darlene, their
faces shimmers of desire. We slip
through the marble mouth of the hospital.
Waving, she calls "Bye-bye, baby."
"Bye-bye, baby," I call back.

Elevatored,
I ascend into hell where
old and mad, the woman sits,
tattered years draped around her shoulders,
all those years,
all one now, but too worn to keep her warm.
"My brain," she says, "has grown wings,
has flown away. I'm waiting for a ride
to take me where it flew."

To My Body

In this world I wear you like a coat,
To my heart, I say
you were broken but you mended over,
glazed and cracked like a china plate, but mended.
To my bones, I say,
you moved, sometimes when you could not.
To my legs, I say,
you walked me through my little life,
through gaudy autumns when the world was painted like
    a gypsy;
through bony winters;
to the mists of green and yellow springs.
To my long gone womb, I say,
you eased out my infants,
almost,
but not quite,
easily.
To my brain, I say,
you teased out a few lines, a few
glass-bottled messages to throw into the oceans of the
    earth.
I knew if I lost my sorrow, I would lose my soul.
To my eyes, I say,
you let me see the beautiful others in my life.
To my stuttering muscles and my misfiring nerves, I say
you are not all of me.
I say to you, my body,
once beloved,
I will shed you like a garment,
and rise.

Return

When the prodigal son returned home,
he sat in the parlor weaving stories.
Everyone was rapt, especially the young girls,
The good son stayed in the kitchen,
muttering and scrubbing.
Pans in which the fatted calf are cooked
are hard to clean.

Career Change

When the woman at the well returned home
after her long talk with the stranger,
she burned her silver sandals and her
perfumed sheets and tacked a sign on her door
that said, "Sewing and Alterations."

Celebrate

holiness of slugs, snails,
worms, all small, crawling
slicks of wonder,
cosmos, yellow dotted daisies,
bush aswarm with drunkenness
of butterfly, blurred
whir of humming bird,
Mr. Lincoln roses
beetle jeweled,
red as satin hearts we sent last winter
on the feast of Valentine,
last night's baseball heroes
hitting homers
over pumpkin colored moon.

September.

1945

On my way to the Rex Theater
alone on a Sunday afternoon
I passed that other sanctuary
Blessed Sacrament Church
with its stone Jesus statue
in the front yard and in the back yard
stone Mary, his mother,
patiently waiting for her May procession
stone snakes beneath her feet,
church door ajar on blackness
clots of candle light
murmur of kneeling women
fingering rosaries
praying for husbands, sons
fighting and dying
in places not even named in atlases.

I sat in the almost empty
movie house, watched Gene Kelly,
Judy Garland, smiling, singing,
dancing until a newsreel
unrolled on the screen—
a European death camp—
a jumbled heap of skin-covered skeletons
tossed in a pit like junk
inhumanly angled
starved, sexless, bald,
eyes staring, wide open
mouths torn apart in soundless
shrieks.

I ran my twelve-year-old
terror home to a house
cold, because there was no coal.
The grandmother was kneading a tub
of white grease in a bowl with a packet
of orange powder making wartime butter.
Cabbage and potatoes simmered
on the stove.

"Nobody screamed," I said.
"Nobody in the whole movie house screamed."
"Sit, eat," she said.

Coconut

In the late thirties before the war,
I was given in my Christmas stocking,
a few peppermints,
tangerines, English walnuts,
and a coconut,
brown, hairy,
with three dark depressions
in its roundness.
They made its monkey face.
The coconut stretched the Christmas stocking,
one of my stepmother's silk stockings,
and it was a long stretch
to reach the treats inside.
My stepmother cut open the coconut.
I was given the thin white milk in a jelly glass.
Its sweetness was Christmas.
The coconut meat was
rich. A small piece appeased the appetite.
The rest of the coconut meat my stepmother grated
and added to the white icing of a white layer cake
she made, a cake magical and white as snow.
With it we ate snow if any fell,
snow flavored with sugar and vanilla.

Two decades later in a movie,
an English commander is shut up in a flat-roofed tin box
and left to bake in the fiery Burma sun
because he insists the Japanese colonel
in charge of the prison camp
follow the Geneva Convention rules on the treatment of
    captives.
A doctor somehow is able to give the dying commander

a coconut. The commander drinks the milk, eats the
　　　white flesh,
survives.
In the theater,
I was eight again,
tasting mercy.

Child's Drawing

Spoked sun its centerpiece,
sky an awning stripe of royal blue,
marshmallow clouds,
birds V'd black, upside down,
square house, triangle-hatted,
no windows,
white path a waterfall down the center of the picture,
tulips, red, purple, yellow
lollipops stuck on stems,
grass a green mat
after thought,
tiny stick-figured mommy
curlicues for hair;
tiny, stick-figured daddy,
with four-fingered hands, dangling;
child between them,
taller than the house,
his smile a scimitar.

Children

Swarms of children surrounded the healer,
climbed on his shoulders,
hung around his waist,
and dragged at his legs.
Others stood at the edge of the crowd,
crying and longing to touch him.
The healer's followers wanted to drive them away.
They were tired and hungry,
They had far to go.
"No," said the healer
"Let them stay.
Heaven is full of children.
To enter Heaven you must be children.
Even you and I must be children."

Anatomy

Before I was married, I had never seen
a naked male except the man
on the metal table
in the Hopkins morgue.
He was unmarked in any way,
beautiful,
not in the manner of a slim Greek statue,
but heavy with muscle, well fed,
a Michelangelo, Adam,
a full-lipped sleeper in a dream of death.
I could look when they made the incision,
throat to pubis,
but when the whirring bone saw cut off
the top of his head
like a knife through cheese,
the room filled with black water.
I passed out.

I was seventeen
an after school typist,
unpaid, at Hopkins to learn
medical terminology, in training
for a halfway promised
job after high school graduation.

It is well known: life is a play
with a trite script,
stereotypical characters,
crude foreshadowing.

Years later,
on our honeymoon,
I turned, just as my husband
stepped out of the shower
in a gleam of nakedness.
Then I remembered
that other nakedness.

25 March 2003

Shimmering,
spring hangs from the trees
in flicks and flecks of gold.
Purple and red are splashed across
the blue silk sky.
Christ will not come
to lead us barefoot
down York road.
The first dead are arriving
at Dover, Delaware,
some of them dead
from friendly fire.
There is no friendly fire.
Between basketball games
and ads for cars and cola
we watch the war.
Staring from the TV screen
American POWs, one of them,
a woman, a cook.
Her family says she loves to cook.

Animals

I have a horse in my bathroom.
I don't know why he stays.
I don't feed him any more.

Everybody thinks the brown bear
is stuffed, lacks
a heart's necessary noise.
I know better. He is real.
More real than they.
Or I.

As the Madagascar
aye-aye left the room
on his little finger feet,
I saw his glass eyes
fill with tears.

When night puts on her satin shawl
with its long fringes falling
to earth, let me creep
under the shawl as a field mouse.
Then let that soundless
air sweeper, Owl, catch me
in his claws, fly me with him
through the rattle trap trees
until he tires. Then let him
loose from his grip
whatever it is
I have become.

Another Christmas

Now call down Christ on this December day,
but not with Revelation's trumpet dooms,
or armored angels bright in rich array
of scarlet cloth from Heaven's spinning looms.
No fear of smitten suns or broken moons,
or seas aflame, or darkened stars dismay
that time he reappears as flesh. Let June's
white roses bloom through winter's dark decay.
But let him come as carpenter or feast
assembler, bread and fish for all; for all
the water walker calming storms, the least
heart's healer, and the one the dead hear call.
And let him come as infant as of old.
The story, told and told, is still untold.

Gratitude

After the loaves and the fishes
had been eaten, there were some who demanded
fresh fruit, white wine,
and linen napkins

Feast

Sitting on an iron bench
outside the hospital waiting
for a taxi on a cool October
morning, hearing overhead
aircraft, maybe Iraq-directed,
I watch the old black man
shuffle his uniform out the hospital door.
He carries a bag of bread crumbs,
whistles shrilly. Sparrows flutter
in the snow of dried crusts.
Crows plod through in black serge suits,
shiny with use, devour all
they can. They have run out of road kill.
The sparrows stay.
From lemon, lime and raspberry lollipop trees,
cardinals fly off in princes' raiment.
They do not join the rabble.
Crows bumble into air.
In their dirty dresses,
puffs of appetite on skinny legs,
sparrows eat and eat. They know
God's eye
is on them.

Birth

From womb and wound
(jagged perineal tear)
a grappling hook
grasped my son's
tender, new-made temples,
dragged him from my belly.

Red placental plop.

Obstetrician grinning,
"You've messed up my hundred dollar
shoes," handed me the child
wrapped up like a loaf of bread—
his scream, his naked monkey's
scarlet face, his button-sized fists
feebly beating the indifferent
air (blood everywhere)
his legs frog-kicking
in an absent sea.

And I, howling and laughing
held at last the six pound
lump of life, his heart
a firecracker popping in his
skinny chest.

February 1947

Reading how Raskolnikov, student,
killed the old woman for money,
I stood at sixteen, lipsticked, high heeled,
at seven A.M., on the corner of Forrest and Hillen
across the street from the Maryland State Penitentiary,
clutching *Crime and Punishment,* a paper-bagged
sandwich, and a pair of boots in case of sudden snow,
waiting for a bus to grumble up from Curtis Bay,
wheeze me to my lab job at Hopkins.
Sweaty night shift Beth Steel stokers
smoked and snored in the back of the bus.
One by one, neon bar signs blinked out down the blocks.
At Wolfe and Monument, I was unloaded
into a reek of sour shit seeping from the perforated
bowel inside the building. Post mortem,
Broadway Jesus stretched out his marble arms
blocks away. Down here stink bloomed in the halls.
Bone saws whined behind swinging doors.
Barely breathing, I ran up five flights
to the desk where I typed the logs
of that day's diseases. On shelves behind me
bumpy wombs wobbled in bowls of fixative.
Exploded ovaries—jelly fish in jars—
swam when anyone walked near them. I never looked
at the six-month fetuses afloat in glass globes
turning and bobbing in formaldehyde every time
a truck rumbled down Wolfe Street.
I thought about Sonya going with Rasknolnikov
to the knife-edged winds and the endless
night snows of Siberia—
for love.

Side Effects

(One of the side effects of Parkinson medication is
hallucinations.)

When I turned on the kitchen light
an inch-long goldfish was swimming
in the cat's aluminum water dish,
slow and easy, round and round.
Through the kitchen window
the Japanese maple stood covered
with quivering cardinals' wings,
so red they looked raw.
Under the tree my grandmother sat
at a rust speckled metal table.
She was peeling apples. She had
taken off her coffin clothes, put on
gold and purple.
"Sit down," she said. "I have crossed
the black satin river no one crosses twice.
We'll make a pie."

First Love

Through those long Sunday rides to Carroll County
to Cousin Reuben's farm,
wearing a white hair ribbon as big as my head,
shelved on the back seat like a suitcase,
I stared at the picture book countryside
stretched outside the car windows:
green fields, brown stripes, curls of fairy tale forest,
red barns, white houses with strips of purple flowers
under the windows; overhead the wide blue sky where
God walked in his gardens, looking down at our
    Plymouth
through holes in the white clouds.
Hadn't they said in Sunday School that God saw
    everything?
Didn't he walk in the graveyard I passed every day going
    to school?
He was dressed in a white nightgown like his pictures
in Sunday School, and smiling and waving.
I asked Daddy and Mom each time we drove out to the
    country,
wasn't God in the graveyard? Did he ride the streetcar
    with us
to Lexington Market? There was an old man who rode the
    streetcar
and he had a little beard like the goat in Druid Hill Park,
    and
eyes with yellow rims.
They never answered.
But God did not come with us to Cousin Reuben's farm.
I loved Cousin Reuben's farm.
I loved Cousin Reuben's shiny black and white cows.
I loved their long, mournful moos.

I thought their whole bodies
were full of white foam,
ear tips to tails,
that their tails were a kind of handle
Cousin Reuben pulled on to make
them empty milk into the silver buckets
lined along the barn wall.
I loved those cows and their long lashes.
In sixth grade I fell in love
with a brown-eyed boy
because he had the same big, sad eyes
and the same eyelashes
cast shadows on his cheeks.

Housekeeper

Martha yearned to sit and talk with Mary
and the man who could raise the rotting dead.
But all her dishes and pans were dirty.
There was no one else to clean.

Getting Older

I didn't mind it too much.
It was like
putting on a skinny coat
you pick up in a second hand store.
When you try it on
it doesn't look as worn
as you thought it would.
It almost fits.

Harry

Dragged by his mower's green striping
roar he stumbles over the lawn
at twilight, lets the black machine
shiver into silence, leans his cardiac
stutter on a maple tree
for a moment, huffs into the house,
lights in every window
for someone
a yellow electric candle.
Moon pours cream across the dark cup
of night. Star grains scatter around its edges.
Harry pulls his brown
guitar from a corner
brushes away tremors of spider webs
strums, sings, "In my heart
you are written in roses
but the writing
was done with thorns."

Graduation, 1949

Seniors in cashmere pastels and pearls
flowed down the high school corridors
in perfume stolen from their
mothers' cut glass bottles bought in France,
and forbidden in the hallways
of this all-girls' school,
but forgiven now by the ghosts of old girls
in charge of us, because these were
the almost women, soon to surrender
their golden page boy haircuts and their tall
white bodies to a tuxedo at a High Mass
wedding choked with flowers,
soprano singing, "Ave Maria,"
bride presenting her baby's breath
and rose bouquet to the Blessed Virgin,
music pouring through the pews
and over the rented red aisle carpet,
all the mothers weeping.

Those of us, bespectacled, and with acne-bitten
faces followed our stolid ankles
to offices. There we sat tapping
day after day, in the Morse code of monotony:
correspondence, reports, reviews.
Sometimes we left our glasses home,
haunted YWCA dance classes,
church socials, night school courses
in accounting, sometimes a better bar,
squinting behind bravado cigarettes,
at somebody male, anybody male,
longing for romance,
a little love.

Honeymoon

We moved our clothes in and our books.
You pulled the "Sold" sign from the rusty August lawn.
We had a kitchen table, two chairs,
a can of chicken noodle soup, a double bed.
We closed the cracked Venetian blinds
the other owner left behind, went to bed
at three in the afternoon, got up in the late
gold day, ate soup, walked
down York Road to where the muddy farmer
offered watermelon, sweet flesh sweating
pink, corn with rows of kernels even
as infant teeth.
We took our country pleasures
daily, planted peonies, roses, crocuses,
so sure, so sure
of next year's spring. You wore
an old straw hat, knees-out khaki's
from one of your wars. At night
we lay in the back yard on a yellow
blanket, waited for Heaven's customary
light show, emptied our coffee
on the ground, libation to the gods.

New Leaves

When the drunkard, staggering home at dawn,
after a three-day spree,
saw the young man walking on water,
he swore
never to touch another drop.

Memorial Day

Blazing down aluminum fences
climbing roses. Red.
Red, white, blue flags
snapping in the wind
along Padonia Road.
Red, black-masked
cardinals called out,
flinging nets of notes
from oak to oak.
Early morning sky. White.
Blue dye of day colored
windowed corners of the world.
White clouds unraveling
in distant trees
Green cemetery. Speckled red, white,
blue with plastic flowers, red
ribboned Styrofoam crosses.
White haired VFW band
trailed bag piped
"Amazing Grace"
past black pond.
White swan afloat.
We drove past.
Car shadow followed. Black.
Four of us.
Red bricks. School.
We parked. Four of us.
White oval running track.
Mile. He ran one mile.
Our children waited in their
red and blue kindergarten clothes,
blue and red second grader clothes.

We had promised them parades.
He ran one mile. Clutched his chest.
Dropped.
And it was all over.

Sons

I

In June the teacher presented
him with the second grade semester project,
a Black Wolf spider, crouching in a round
aquarium, its eight legs dancing up for flies.
The spider sat in the boy's room half a summer,
its glassed in face aghast with eyes, lima bean
body wearing away its spidery fatness until the
boy decided, "Wolfie is losing weight.
He's homesick. He wants the woods."

In a stand of trees the spider slid from its
turned over prison, vanished.
The boy waved.
For a long time he waited for the spider to reappear,
signal some goodbye.

II

Green as a lucky shamrock
the garter snake curled in a wooden cage
the boy had bought for a dollar from
a friend whose mother screamed at snakes.
Tenderly, the boy filled the snake's water
dish, fed it worms not much bigger than
parentheses.
It was hard to keep that snake fed.
Even the grandmother pulled up
rocks from her garden, gathered piles

of wriggling pink to keep the snake from starving.
The child saved the snake's slipped off skins
in his underwear drawer.
When the snake shed its six-inch length of life,
the boy smeared away his tears,
buried it in a shoebox.

The Second Coming

We set our plastic chairs along the road three days ago,
knowing they were safe; no one would steal anybody's
    place.
This is a nice neighborhood, after all.
Some of us wanted to see the show.
Some of us had serious business with the guy coming up
    the road.
We had heard things. He was on TV.
On national TV.
We had thermos jugs and cheese sandwiches in paper
    bags.
We were on waiting lists for transplants
or at the least for major surgeons.
We needed new organs.
We were deaf, dumb, blind and mad,
The rest of us,
I swear to God, one old man brought a hearse with his
    dead daughter in it.
There were no beautiful people waiting there.
Meantime, a little man came down the road
with a trail of honking horns behind him.
A cop car came up and asked to see the little man's
    parade permit.
His friends straggled between the trucks and the SUVs.
They were all hot and thirsty.
The leader had wild eyes, what color you couldn't say.
He was mumbling something.
He was thin. His ribs showed through his ragged flannel
    shirt,
his jeans were torn at the knees. He had a scarf tied
    around his head.
Once in a while he tore it off and wiped his face.

He looked like a sixties hippy,
but, of course, this was the second millennium.
Some people tried to touch him, reach out, you know,
but he shrugged them off, or he held out his hand
for a handout and the guys with him were asking for
    money outright.
Some of them were tattooed.
It was embarrassing.

The Pitcher

God loves baseball.
But sometimes He switches sides.
Last year's Cy Young winner,
riding the crowd, a golden surfer
on a legendary wave, this year
walks the first three batters, balks, pitches wild.
Meanwhile, his own men—
one
two
three—
strike out.
He surrenders the ball
in the bottom of the third.
He would rather chop his chest apart,
pull out his own exasperated heart,
than hand over the stitched sphere
sweating in his palm.
Dropping in the dugout like a stone,
he curses, spits, twists the gold
chain around his neck, feels chilled,
stuffs his not quite numb wrist,
elbow ache, shoulder stiffness
in his warm-up jacket,
closes his marksman's eyes,
mutters, "Never mind.
It ain't over 'til it's over."

Trade Off

After the young man heard
that to enter Heaven he had to surrender
his home in the south of France,
his several yachts, and his platinum watches,
he drove home in his Mercedes
to swim in his pool,
and think it over.

Love in Another City

You always wore your tipsy crown
like any king
and commandeered the hearts
of all the girls who knew you then.
I was one.
It was not your profile silhouetted
dark that day against the darker rain
or your eyes so little boy blue or
the smiles you handed out
like paid for autographs.
All of that was just
the passing by of butterflies.
It was something in you made
us want to heal you
even as you disappeared
into one of those Baltimore
bars where the smell of beer
hung outside on the sidewalk
thick as bricks and where going in the door
was going into darkness
and those "Baby, baby" blues songs
groaned all night long.

Sunflowers

One morning you and I
counted twenty black
and yellow finches feeding
on sunflowers
tall as circus stiltmen.
Startled
the finches flew away
all at once, a little curtain
flipping in the sky.

In other ages lovers swore
that at their deaths their
buried bodies ought to feed
April gloried trees or twin
red rose vines climbing
the air to ease around
each others' thorns.

But you and I, when
we are done
let us give our flesh to feed
those citizens of sun
on whose black and yellow flowers
greedy singers cling
gobbling seeds to fuel
flight and song.

Moving Day

We packed china
and pictures
carried out beds
with the dead still in them.
Until then
we had never moved
the grandfather's clock
made in Libertytown
circa seventeen fifty-six.
All that was left of us
when we locked the door
was a painted over oblong
on the wall
where the clock had stood
its tick the tap
of a blind man's cane.

Nocturne

You know how it is,
You wake up at 2:17 A.M. and right away you know
Macbeth hath murdered sleep.
An icy moon glares through the glass.
Close the curtain. Find some way to sleep.
The books of the Bible are long gone.
The alphabet, forward and backward, too easy.
The mind drifts and finds again what awakened it.
2:48 A.M. Name the states in alphabetical order,
Over and over and still forget one or two.
Instead, recite cities and states. Too easy.
Make a list of authors, English or American by birth,
but Balzac creeps in and Tolstoy. You wish that
you could write one paragraph, one sentence like theirs.
  Your eyes
open staring at the ceiling where someone has
written "Failure" in flaming letters. And your
face burns. Your brittle heart cracks again.
3:22 A.M. Dredge up every poem you learned
by heart. 3:46 A.M. You can't recall that many.
Your mind escapes into the forest of memory,
digs up every body buried there, replays every
  blundering
word you spoke there. 4:12 A.M. Worst of all!,
What you said to him today, or is it now
yesterday? You presumed too much. You saw too late
his pupils narrow and a tightness in his lips.
4:17 A.M. You try to think of Bible verses, but the only
one that comes to mind is, "Thy faith hath made thee
  whole."
But you have no faith.
4:30 A.M. You fall into a sleep

so heavy, even sleeping, you feel drugged. Something
creeps around the room, ready to kill you and you
scream, "Mother, mother." She appears next to the bed.
The creature vanishes. You don't want to say it, but you
    do.
"I love you, Mother. Please forgive me." She disappears.
4:47 A.M. Your remember what you said to him. So
    presumptuous.
What a fool you are, 5:02 A.M. You crumble into sleep.
There he stands. He says, "Stop sending me these
messages." You don't dream any more. 5:20 A.M.
You stand. You pull the curtain. Tired of waiting,
the moon has slicked away. Dawn drags its dirty
rags across the window.

One more morning.

Second-Go-Round

After the dead man rose from the dead
he sold his pottery, packed his clothes
and boarded a camel, swearing to see the world
before he had to leave it again

Sundays

After the sermon on love and forgiveness,
the heavenly music,
and the passing of peace
the attendees sprint to the parking lot,
jump into their vehicles,
and with horns blasting,
and fists waving,
race away.

Six A.M.

Grandfather's clock is ticking.
(Now that I am older, I hardly hear it.)
Its face is dirty.
The engine of its sun has erred.
Its metal moon is broken.

I have stopped assigning chores
to its every marked off minute.

Outside, the real moon moves down,
a blossom trailing silver.
The sun, on stage as always,
performs each day its same magician's trick.
Pulls its curly fire-edges in,
transforms itself
into an orange circle
wheels away.

Morning comes up clapping in the windy trees.

Rain

Watching the rain fall
on the windows hour after hour.
And the hole in the asphalt road
fill up, spill over, I wait for the letter
that never comes, wait for the call that never comes,
walking in and out of rooms, up and down the stairs, up
and down the halls, longing for another human face,
I slosh out to the car
drowsing in the downpour,
drive to the supermarket
in search of consolation cookies,
frozen chicken pot pie,
candy bars. Leaning down an aisle
on my cart, I discover my sons
from three decades past and stand, stunned,
watching the older one, dark haired,
tall for seven, drop his arm
around his smaller brother's shoulder
as they reach for plastic cars on racks,
toy binoculars, baseballs,
all apples in their double-Adam'ed Eden.
Then they turn, become
somebody else's boys.

Years ago, after their father's funeral,
weeks of rain,
on a June day, bright with brides,
invited to spend the day with friends,
the older one's arm
around his brother's shoulder,
dragging shadows after them,
they walked away,
disappeared down the street.

Origin

Ugly with a big head full of eyes,
a prisoner's hair cut, thirteen,
I knew no one would ever love me;
walked to school to the rhythm
of iambic pentameter, hating
and loving the City College boys
on the corner in their brand new beards.
I wanted a Romeo the way a long
distance runner wants water, the way
a drunk wants whiskey. The only
thing I had to offer no one wanted:
words. Heavy as rocks they roared
in my head, begging to escape. Nobody
wanted them, certainly not I, but they
came out anyway, as everywhere as air.